Extreme Sports Facts

by Noah Leatherland

Minneapolis, Minnesota

Credits

Images are courtesy of Shutterstock.com. With thanks to Getty Images, Thinkstock Photo, Alamy, and iStockphoto. Background pattern – Dmitry Kostrov. Cover – nicemonkey, deeg, Sira Anamwong, zigzag design, Nikolai V Titov, Jtoybox, Depot Visual, GN.Studio. 4–5 – Macrovector, Mind Pixell, oneinchpunch, Photobac. 6–7 – Alexander Ryabintsev, Guy Kawasaki: File-WorldDogSurfingChampionship2016-15.jpg, inspiring.team, Jonathan Mitchell Images, Mascha Tace, Zuma Press, Inc.. 8–9 – Bernhard: https://en.wikipedia.org/wiki/Mega_ramp#/media/File-Freestyle.ch_2004_sonnenuntergang.jpg, ivector, lemono, Martin Charles Hatch, robuart. 10–11 – Christian Bertrand, Glyph_stock, GROGL, MsuperDESIGN, OKREATIF DIGITAL. 12–13 – Flystock, GoodStudio, Ipatov, Lucky clover. 14–15 – Danny Iacob, GN.Studio, VectorShow, VectorsMarket. 16–17 – Macrovector, Samsul Said, Sergii Figurnyi, Sinesp. 18–19 – HappyPictures, Rick Neves, Sinesp. 20–21 – Frolova_Elena, hurricanehank, NotionPic. 22–23 – denayunebgt, Iuliia Khramtsova, lukpedclub, Mauro Rodrigues, travelview. 24–25 – Look_Studio, lukpedclub, Microgen, Paolo Bona, pikepicture. 26–27 – Almazoff, Macrovector, Mind Pixell, Photobac, ThulungPhoto.com. 28–29 – a katz, EPG_EuroPhotoGraphics, IrinaChevzhik, mejorana, Valentina Vectors. 30 – BNP Design Studio, Mind Pixell, PeopleImages.com - Yuri A.

Bearport Publishing Company Product Development Team

President: Jen Jenson; Director of Product Development: Spencer Brinker; Managing Editor: Allison Juda; Associate Editor: Naomi Reich; Associate Editor: Tiana Tran; Art Director: Colin O'Dea; Designer: Kim Jones; Designer: Kayla Eggert; Product Development Assistant: Owen Hamlin

Library of Congress Cataloging-in-Publication Data is available at www.loc.gov or upon request from the publisher.

ISBN: 979-8-89232-068-9 (hardcover)
ISBN: 979-8-89232-542-4 (paperback)
ISBN: 979-8-89232-201-0 (ebook)

© 2025 BookLife Publishing
This edition is published by arrangement with BookLife Publishing.

North American adaptations © 2025 Bearport Publishing Company. All rights reserved. No part of this publication may be reproduced in whole or in part, stored in any retrieval system, or transmitted in any form or by any means, electronic, mechanical, photocopying, recording, or otherwise, without written permission from the publisher. Bearport Publishing is a division of Chrysalis Education Group.

For more information, write to Bearport Publishing, 5357 Penn Avenue South, Minneapolis, MN 55419.

CONTENTS

Insane, Wacky Sports 4

Surfing 6

Skateboarding 8

BMX. 10

Snowboarding. 12

Skiing 14

BASE Jumping. 16

Wingsuiting 18

Motocross. 20

Zorbing 22

Boxing. 24

Climbing 26

Eating 28

Stay Safe!. 30

Glossary 31

Index. 32

Read More 32

Learn More Online 32

INSANE, WACKY SPORTS

People love sports. Luckily, there are more than 8,000 sports to chose from.

Some sports are more **extreme** than others. They can send people flying high and climbing to the edge.

Sports can be a lot of hard work. People who take them to the extreme may break **records**.

Let's learn about some insane, wacky sports!

SURFING

Surfing is all about riding the waves.

THE LARGEST SURFBOARD IN THE WORLD HAS TO BE CARRIED BY A FORKLIFT!

Sebastian Steudtner is the record holder for surfing the biggest wave. It was 86 feet (26 m) tall.

Abbie Girl holds the record for longest wave surfed . . . by a dog! She rode it for 352 ft. (107 m).

LOOKS LIKE THE WAVES ARE *RUFF* TODAY!

The first person to surf while on fire was Jamie O'Brien.

SKATEBOARDING

Extreme skateboarding involves going higher and faster than everyone else.

THE HIGHEST HALF-PIPE REACHED 7 FT. (2 M) INTO THE AIR.

The fastest speed on a skateboard was set at 91 miles per hour (146 kph).

The longest distance anyone has traveled while doing a handstand on a skateboard was 2,255 ft. (687 m).

In 2005, Danny Way used a mega ramp to jump over the Great Wall of China on a skateboard.

A MEGA RAMP

THE GREAT WALL OF CHINA

BMX

There are many insane tricks that BMX riders can do on a bike.

MANY BMXS DO NOT HAVE ANY BRAKES. THIS MAKES IT EASIER FOR RIDERS TO DO TRICKS.

How far could you go while backflipping on a BMX? The record is 62 ft. (19 m).

The farthest traveled while doing a manual was 2,127 ft. (648 m).

A MANUAL IS LIFTING THE FRONT WHEEL OF A BIKE OFF THE GROUND WITHOUT PEDALING!

Someone once did 62 bar spins in under a minute. It set a record!

SNOWBOARDING

Extreme snowboarding is when people slide down steep **slopes**.

TRICKS IN THE FREEZING COLD? *BRR!*

The highest speed ever reached on a snowboard was about 125 mph (200 kph).

People do tricks in the air, too! One extreme snowboarder once spun six times in the air.

In 2023, Mia Brookes became the youngest snowboarding world champion in history. She was only 16 years old!

13

SKIING

Skis were **invented** to help people travel across frozen land. Today, some skiers use them to **perform** extreme tricks.

The longest jump ever recorded on a pair of skis was 831 ft. (253 m).

The ski speed record was set at 159 mph (256 kph).

SKUGGLING IS SKIING AND JUGGLING AT THE SAME TIME.

Thomas Petrie holds the world record for skuggling. He did it for 5,250 ft. (1,600 m)!

BASE JUMPING

BASE jumping is when people jump from really high places!

THE BURJ KHALIFA

The highest BASE jump from a building was off the Burj Khalifa. This tower is 2,717 ft. (828 m) tall.

The record for the most BASE jumps in one day is 201.

BASE JUMPERS USE PARACHUTES TO LAND SAFELY.

Miles Daisher has done the most BASE jumps ever. He has more than 4,000 jumps under his belt!

WINGSUITING

Have you ever wanted to fly? Wingsuiting might be the closest thing to it!

The longest time a person spent wingsuiting was 9 minutes and 6 seconds.

Want to set a wingsuit record? You'll have to go faster than 247 mph (397 kph).

SOMETIMES, PEOPLE PUT JETS ON THEIR WINGSUITS TO GO EVEN FASTER!

The highest jump in a wingsuit was from 43,254 ft. (13,184 m).

MOTOCROSS

For some people, motorcycles are just another way to get around. But others like to use them for extreme tricks.

The longest motocross bike jump with a backflip was 65 ft. (20 m).

When someone drives only on the front wheel, it is called a nose wheelie. The longest nose wheelie performed on a motocross bike was 282 ft. (86 m).

RIDERS SPREAD OUT THEIR ARMS AND LEGS WHILE DOING THE HOLY GRAB.

One extreme motocross trick is called the Holy Grab. It is when the rider jumps into the air and lets go of their bike. Then, they must grab hold of the bike again.

ZORBING

Zorbing is a sport where people roll down hills inside zorb balls.

ZORB BALLS ARE BIG INFLATABLE (IN-FLAY-TUH-BUHL) BALLS.

The farthest traveled by zorb ball in a single roll was 1,870 ft. (570 m).

The fastest speed while zorbing was 32 mph (52 kph).

Sometimes, zorbing can be mixed with other sports. People play zorb soccer.

23

BOXING

Boxing is one of the oldest and most extreme sports in the world.

Len Wickwar holds the record for the most boxing matches and wins in a career. He fought in 472 total matches with 342 wins.

In 1893, the longest boxing match lasted more than 7 hours.

THE MATCH WENT MORE THAN 100 ROUNDS.

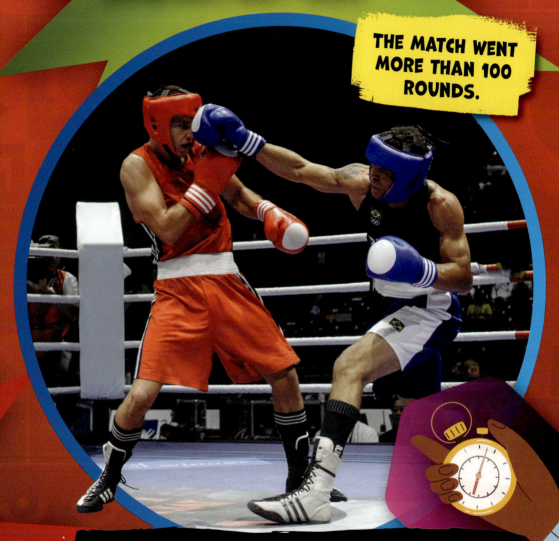

Some boxing matches are over as soon as they start. The fastest knockout in a boxing match was 10 seconds!

CLIMBING

Another extreme sport is climbing. People were doing it for thousands of years before it even became a sport.

ALAIN ROBERT

Alain Robert holds the record for climbing the most buildings. He has made his way up more than 100 buildings, including towers and skyscrapers.

In a hurry? Speed climbing is all about climbing fast. The fastest a person climbed up a 50 ft. (15 m) wall was 4.9 seconds.

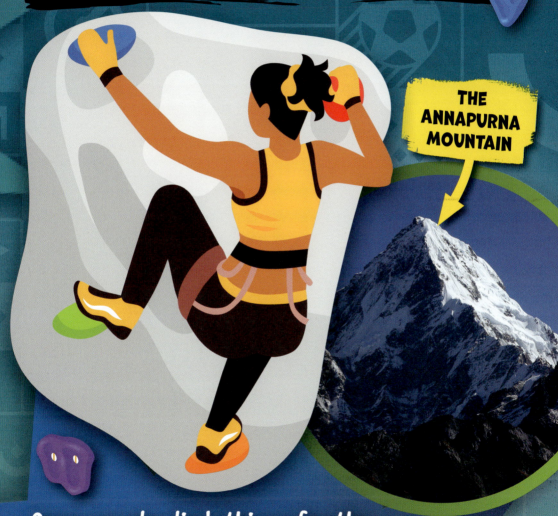

THE ANNAPURNA MOUNTAIN

Some people climb things for the danger. While the Annapurna is not the tallest mountain in the world, it is known for having deadly **avalanches**.

EATING

Even eating can be extreme.

Joey Chestnut holds more than 50 world records for eating. He is best known for eating 76 hot dogs in 10 minutes!

JOEY CHESTNUT

28

Sometimes, extreme eating adds something else into the mix.

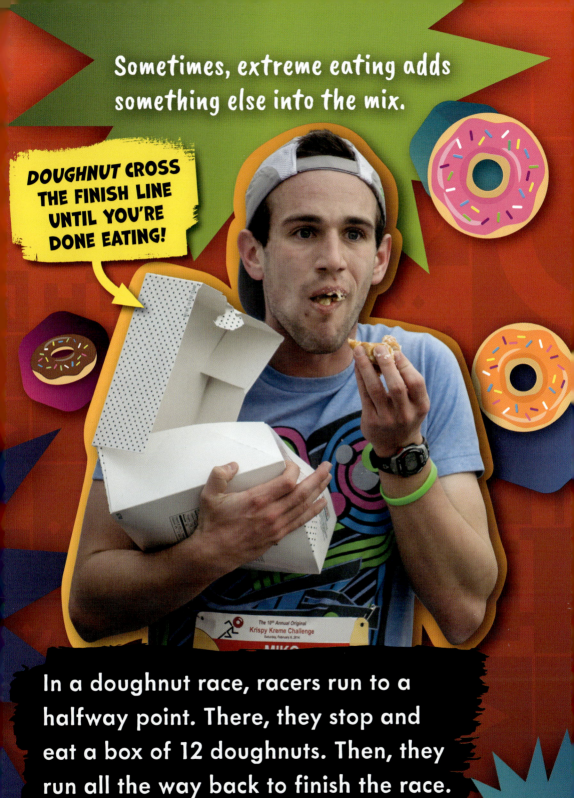

DOUGHNUT CROSS THE FINISH LINE UNTIL YOU'RE DONE EATING!

In a doughnut race, racers run to a halfway point. There, they stop and eat a box of 12 doughnuts. Then, they run all the way back to finish the race.

29

STAY SAFE!

From surfing to wingsuiting, the world is full of cool and sometimes dangerous sports. That's what makes them extreme!

Extreme sports take a lot of practice. People who do them put in lots of work to make sure they stay as safe as possible.

GLOSSARY

avalanches large amounts of snow, ice, or dirt that break off and move down mountains at fast speeds without warning

extreme at the highest level with an element of risk

half-pipe a ramp that curves at both ends to create a U-shape

inflatable something that can be filled with air

invented made for the first time

perform to carry out an action in front of an audience

records the best achievements in a certain skill

slopes lines or surfaces with one end higher than the other

INDEX

backflips 10, 20
bikes 10–11, 20–21
doughnuts 29
motorcycles 20
races 29
skateboards 8–9
skis 14–15
snowboards 12–13
surfboards 6
waves 6–7
wingsuits 18–19, 30
zorbing 22–23

READ MORE

Flynn, Brendan. *Extreme Sports GOATs: The Greatest Athletes of All Time (Sports Illustrated Kids: GOATs).* North Mankato, MN: Capstone Press, 2024.

Kaiser, Brianna. *Weird Sports (Wonderfully Weird. Alternator Books).* Minneapolis: Lerner Publications, 2024.

LEARN MORE ONLINE

1. Go to **www.factsurfer.com** or scan the QR code below.
2. Enter "**Sports Facts**" into the search box.
3. Click on the cover of this book to see a list of websites.